REPORT OF COMMITTEE

ON

COURSES OF STUDY AND FACULTY

FOR THE

ILLINOIS INDUSTRIAL UNIVERSITY.

PUBLISHED BY ORDER OF THE BOARD OF TRUSTEES.

SPRINGFIELD:
BAKER, BAILHACHE & CO., PRINTERS.
1867.

REPORT OF COMMITTEE

ON

COURSES OF STUDY AND FACULTY

FOR THE

ILLINOIS INDUSTRIAL UNIVERSITY.

PUBLISHED BY ORDER OF THE BOARD OF TRUSTEES.

Inasmuch as some time must necessarily elapse before the University can be properly equipped and prepared for opening, the committee present now, only the outlines and some of the general features of a plan of organization, hoping to be permitted, by fuller consultation with each other, and with eminent educators in other States, who are engaged in organizing similar institutions, to ripen their plans more fully before presenting them in detail. In laying the foundations of an institution which is to last through coming ages, and to affect all future generations, we have need to plan wisely. We must not expose ourselves, needlessly, to the inconveniences of changes, nor to suspicions of caprice.

THE GENERAL AIMS OF THE UNIVERSITY.

The aims of any institution necessarily control its organization. It should be fitted to its uses. The great general aims of the University are defined by the statutes under which it is established. Though not strictly confined by law to the objects proposed in the congressional grant, we are yet bound to meet those objects fully and fairly. According to the language of the grant, "the leading object shall be, without excluding other scientific and classical studies, and including military tactics, to teach such branches of learning as are related to agriculture and the mechanic arts, in order to promote the liberal and practical education of the industrial classes, in the several pursuits and professions in life."

Or, changing the order of statement, the chief aim of the University is, "*the liberal and practical education of the industrial classes*, in the several pursuits and professions in life;" and in order to this end, the University is "to teach such branches of learning as are related to agriculture and the mechanic arts, without excluding other scientific and classical studies, and including military tactics." The military tactics are required, and the scientific and classical studies are permitted. Such at least is the common construction of these clauses, though the language may not unreasonably be understood to imply that the latter studies *shall not* be excluded from the course.

The State law evidently aims to carry out the intention of the congressional grant, and gives the trustees power "to appoint such professors and instructors, and establish and provide for the management of such model farms, model art and other departments, as may be required to teach, in the most thorough manner, such branches of learning as are related to agriculture and the mechanic arts, and military tactics, without excluding other scientific and classical studies." This slight change of the order of the language of the congressional enactment, gives additional emphasis to the opinion that it was intended to prohibit the exclusion of other scientific and classical studies. Under any construction, the Legislature evidently intended to insist—as the law of Congress insists—on the industrial and military education, yet explicitly allowing the trustees to enlarge the scope of studies as they may see fit.

A clearer insight into the real intention of the congressional grant may be gained if we call to mind that the Colleges, existing at the time of the passage of the act making this grant, were adapted only to fit men for the so-called "learned professions," and that the influence of these colleges tended to withdraw their students from the pursuits of industry. Congress therefore proposed to create a new class of colleges, which should train men for industrial pursuits, and help to turn some portion of the great currents of educated life into the channels of industry. They aimed to link learning more closely to labor, and to bring the light of science more fully to the aid of the productive arts. Any other interpretation of the design of Congress than this would involve an absurdity.

The Industrial College was not an expression of congressional condemnation of the ordinary college, or opposition to it. A grant of a township of land in each new State had already provided for State Universities of the common sort. And besides these, rich and powerful seats of learning were every where fitting men for the great public fields of Law, Medicine and Theology. Congress only sought to extend still wider the benefits of science and liberal culture. They wished to establish other seats of learning, equally great and equally powerful, which should send scholars of high scientific attainments and broad and liberal culture, to the farms and workshops of the country.

And finally, as it was not the object of the Industrial Colleges to educate simply the sons of farmers and mechanics, so it was not their design to teach the mere manual arts of agriculture and manufacture. The college course can not replace the apprenticeship in the shop or on the farm; and if it could, a hundred such universities as this could not train to their various trades the future farmers and mechanics of this State. Some practice should, if possible, accompany the scientific study of the several arts, but the aim of this practice must be to insure the thorough comprehension of the principles involved. To teach the millions their trades, however desirable, is beyond our power. To so teach the few who will come and patiently complete their course, that they shall be thorough masters of practical science, and able in their turn to teach others, this is the worthy and attainable end of the University.

The committee profoundly appreciate and commend the far-reaching wisdom and beneficence of these aims of the congressional grant, and would seek to carry them out to the very letter. They have discussed thus fully the intent of the congressional enactment, in order to brush aside the false impressions which may have gained currency, and to bring out into clearer relief this grand idea of the Industrial University, as it lies involved in both State and national statutes—a true University organized in the interest of the industrial, rather than of the professional pursuits, and differing from other Universities in that its departments are technological rather than professional—schools of Agriculture and Art, rather than schools of Medicine and Law. Its central educational courses, while equally broad and liberal, are to be selected to fit men for the study and mastery of the great branches of industry, rather than to serve as introductions to the study of law, medicine, or theology.

This broad idea of the Industrial University proceeds upon the two fundamental assumptions: First, that the agricultural and mechanical arts are the peers of any others in their dignity, importance and scientific scope: and, Second, that the thorough mastery of these arts, and of the sciences applicable to them, requires an education different in kind, but as systematic and complete as that required for the comprehension of the learned professions. It thus avoids the folly of offering as leaders of progress in the splendid industries of the nineteenth century, men of meager attainments and stinted culture, and steers clear also of that other and absurder folly of supposing that mere common school boys, without any thorough discipline, can successfully master and apply the complicated sciences which enter into and explain the manifold processes of modern agriculture and mechanic art.

Nor is it forgotten that man is something more than the artisan, and that manhood has duties and interests higher and grander than those of the workshop and the farm. Education must fit for society and citizenship, as well as for science and industry. The educated agriculturist and mechanic will not unfrequently be called to serve in Senate chambers and gubernatorial chairs, and will need an education broader and better than the simple knowledge of his art.

The State has need every where, but especially in the center and at the head of the great industries on which, as on corner stones, rest down her material progress and power, of broad-breasted, wise-hearted, clear-thinking men—men of rich, deep culture, and sound education.

And besides all this, it should be reflected that half the public value of a body of educated and scientific agriculturists and mechanicians will be lost, if they lack the literary culture which will enable them to communicate, through the press, or by public speech, their knowledge and discoveries; or if they are wanting in that thorough discipline which will make them active and competent investigators and inventors, long after their school days are over.

Nor would we forget, nor attempt by a one-sided education to restrain, that free movement and versatility of American life and genius which leads so many of our more eminent citizens to the successive mastery of several vocations. Let us educate for life, as well as for art, leaving genius free to follow its natural attractions, and lending to talent a culture fitting it for all the emergencies of public or private duty. If some of our graduates shall quit, for a time, the harvest field for the forum, or prefer medicine to mechanic art, we shall hope they will demonstrate that, even in professional life, the education we give is neither inferior nor inadequate. And in riper years they will return to their first love, and bring their gathered wealth and honors to lay them in the lap of the agriculture and art we have taught them. Let the State open wide, then, this Pierian fount of learning. Let her bid freely all her sons to the full and unfailing flow: those whose thirst or whose needs are little, to what they require; those whose thirst and whose capacities are large, to drink their fill. Let the university be made worthy the great state whose name it bears; worthy the grand and splendid industries it seeks to promote; and worthy of the great century in which we live.

DEPARTMENTS AND COURSES OF INSTRUCTION.

Having thus defined the general idea and aims of the University, the Committee suggest the following enumeration of departments, with the courses of instruction in each:

I. The Agricultural Department—Embracing:

1. The course in Agriculture proper.
2. The course in Horticulture and Landscape Gardening.

II The Polytechnic Department—Embracing:

1. The course in Mechanical Science and Art.
2. The course in Civil Engineering.
3. The course in Mining and Metallurgy.
4. The course in Architecture and Fine Arts.

III. The Military Department—Embracing:

1. The course in Military Engineering.
2. The course in Military Tactics.

IV. The Department of Chemistry and Natúral Science.

V. The Department of Trade and Commerce.

VI. The Department of General Science and Literature—Embracing:

1. The course in Mathematics.
2. The course in Natural History, Chemistry, etc.
3. The course in English Language and Literature.
4. The course in Modern Languages and Literature.
5. The course in Ancient Languages and Literature.
6. The course in History and Social Science.
7. The course in Philosophy, Intellectual and Moral.

It may not be found feasible to develop all these departments at the outset, but ultimately even others may be added to those here enumerated.

The following brief exposition of some of the principal courses will exhibit their general scope:

1. The course in agriculture proper may embrace the study of common tillage, arboriculture, fruit growing, cattle and sheep husbandry, veterinary art, agricultural chemistry, and rural engineering and architecture.

Its aim will be to give a practical knowledge of the various kinds of soils, their composition and improvement, by chemical or by mechanical treatment; the several classes of crops, with the preparation of the soil, seeding, cultivation and harvesting of each; the rotation of crops, and preparation and use of fertilizers; vegetable anatomy and physiology, with the classification, values, and laws of growth and culture of the cereals, grasses, and other useful plants, together with general botany; fruit-growing and the several modes of propagation, and the production of new varieties; arboriculture, with the nature and value of the various species of ornamental, shade and forest trees, the propagation, growth and care of forests, their importance and value in a prairie country, in their effects upon climate, vegetation and health; animal anatomy and physiology, with a study of the breeds of domestic animals, and their values for the dairy, for fattening, for draught, and for wool or other products, and of the principles of stock-breeding; veterinary art, with the laws of feeding, care and training of the domestic animals; the apiary and poultry yard; agricultural chemistry, applied to the analysis of soils, fertilizers and food, etc.; entomology, especially including the useful insects, and those injurious to animal life; meteorology and climatology; rural architecture and engineering, embracing the planning of farm buildings, and the laying out, draining and fencing of farms; political economy, the laws of production, consumption and markets; real estate jurisprudence, the laws regulating the tenures and transfers of land, and the laws relating to rural affairs; the history of agriculture, and general views of the husbandry of foreign countries. To these studies should be added, either to prepare for the foregoing, or as necessary to complete education, courses in mathematics, language and literature, mental and moral philosophy, logic, history and science of government.

The instruction should be partly by text-books, and partly by lectures, enforced by observation and practice in the laboratory, and the various departments of the experimental farm.

2. The course of instruction in horticulture may comprehend most of the studies already described under the course in agriculture, omitting stock-breeding and veterinary art, and adding to the fruit-growing, the culture of the small fruits and culinary vegetables, and the culture of flowers; the construction and management of the hot-bed, the greenhouse, the grapery, the seed-plot and the nursery; landscape gardening, the laying out and ornamentation of public and private pleasure grounds, parks, cemeteries, etc. The methods of instruction should be like those in the department of agriculture.

3. The courses in mechanics, civil engineering and mining belong properly to the polytechnic school. All the fundamental sciences involved in them being taught at the University, these courses may also be developed there. The committee defer the delineation of a course of instruction in this department till the question of the extent of its means of development is settled.

4. Military tactics being specifically required by the act of Congress, the development of this department to such an extent as may be found practicable, should be undertaken at the outset. While the effect of this department will be to scatter through the state a body of men so far advanced in military art that, in case of war, they will furnish skillful officers, ready to drill and lead the volunteer forces of the country, it is the opinion of many experienced educators that the introduction of the military drill and discipline is of positive value for their educating influence. They will materially assist in the government of the institution, and tend to form those habits of order and punctuality, for the want of which so many educated men fail of usefulness and success.

It is strongly recommended by eminent military officers, that some simple and tasteful uniform be prescribed for all the students, as the law contemplates and provides; that the organization partake somewhat the military form, and that a daily drill be had in military tactics. The uniform would not be more expensive than ordinary clothing, and its use would repress extravagances in dress, and promote a feeling of democratic equality among the whole body of students. It will help also to stimulate the virtues of personal neatness and manly courtesy of demeanor.

By frequent rotations in office, and by making those eligible to office who merit it by proficiency in drill and by good soldierly conduct, a sufficient stimulus would be gained to insure attention, and both the faculties of obedience and command would be developed. Students of the first year might be required to serve in the ranks and as non-commissioned officers, the higher officers being selected from the advanced classes. Some new drill might also be introduced for each advanced class, and thus the interest be sustained.

Besides the field exercises, some elementary text books should be used, and the students be required to read for recitations or for examinations on the general principles of military science.

It is hoped by the friends of military education that provision will soon be made by congress for the detail of competent officers of the army to act as professors of military science in the colleges introducing it, and that in this way the university may be provided with instructors in this department.

5. The course in chemistry and natural science will embrace the study of analytical and practical chemistry, the analysis of soils, ores, minerals and organic bodies, and the applications of chemistry in agriculture and the arts of dyeing and bleaching, and the manufacture of sugar, salt, glass, etc. It will embrace also the more extended and practical study of mineralogy, geology, and natural history in general, with the arts of collecting and preserving specimens, and of arranging cabinets and conducting geological surveys.

6. The instruction in the department of trade and commerce will have for its aim to give students a knowledge of the principles of business, and of the customs and laws of trade—the collection, transportation, exchange and distribution of the valuable products of nature and art. Such knowledge will be eminently valuable to the educated farmer, and is of vital necessity to those who are to be employed in the great commercial branches of industry. The crowded rooms of the commercial schools, meagre and unscientific as the instruction of these schools often is, prove conclusively the felt need of such a department of instruction, and the university would be incomplete in its industrial courses if it should leave this important form of human industry unprovided for.

The studies in this department, in addition to such literary studies as are necessary for the requisite discipline and culture, and such knowledge of natural sciences as may be needful to an understanding of the origin, nature, quality and cost of the commodities, crude and manufactured, known to commerce, should embrace also political economy, the laws of production, exchange and consumption as they affect markets; the theories of banking, insurance, and foreign and domestic exchange; the laws governing importation and exportation, the several classes of imposts, duties, etc., and the theories connected therewith; commercial geography, with the staple commodities of the different regions and nations, their commercial condition, usages and markets; book-keeping in its several forms, and commercial customs, papers and correspondence; and finally, commercial law and the history of commerce with its growths and variations. Such knowledge, while it would make intelligent business men, farmers, merchants and manufacturers, and managers of the great business enterprises of the nation, would help to prevent those ruinous speculations and disastrous failures which spring as often from a pitiable ignorance of the great fundamental laws of trade, as from a willful violation of them.

DEPARTMENT OF GENERAL SCIENCE AND LITERATURE.

The several courses in this department make up the general educational or college course. Their main aim is to furnish such a liberal education as may best fit students either for the mastery of the special courses in the arts, or for the general duties of life. The final composition and adjustment of this central course will demand the most careful consideration. The conflicting views which prevail as to relative values of different branches of learning, and the consequent disposition to scout some as useless, and to magnify others as of overshadowing importance, make it requisite for us to recur briefly to some fundamental principles which ought to control our selection.

The knowledges considered as instruments of culture or education, may be broadly grouped into four grand divisions, as follows:

1. Natural sciences, or sciences of observation and experiment.
2. Mathematics, or the science of imagination and calculation.
3. Linguistic and philological sciences, or the sciences of formal expression.

4. Philosophical and speculative sciences, or the sciences of consciousness and reflection.

Each form of knowledge affects culture by two separate methods. First, by the kind and extent of the exercise its study affords the mind, and secondly, by the exciting and stimulating effect of its proper ideas. Some studies are chiefly valuable for the former, and others for the latter use.

The natural sciences, or sciences of nature, embracing natural history, chemistry, natural philosophy, geology, physical geography and uranography, especially exercise and cultivate the powers of observation, classification and inductive reasoning.

The mathematical studies, embracing both pure and applied mathematics, exercise and develop the capacity to form and combine abstract conceptions, and cultivate the deductive reason. They also promote habits of mental concentration and continuity of thought.

Linguistic studies educate the discriminative judgment, and develop the power both of the expression and reception of thought. They train also the faculty of discursive reasoning, and help to give to the mental action a precision and clearness not otherwise to be gained.

The philosophical and speculative sciences, embracing mental and moral philosophy, and historical and social science, address themselves to minds already well matured, and powerfully exercise the reflective faculties. They especially develop the habit of looking for the fundamental and essential, in facts and things; of investigating the real nature and causes of social and vital phenomena, and of that reasoning from the contingent and the probable, which goes among us by the name of "common sense."

If we turn now to note the other educational force found in these several classes of knowledge—the stimulating power of their proper ideas—we shall find an equal diversity in the kind and degree of their influence; the philosophical studies being to the majority of mature minds, the most stimulating, and the matematical, the least.

Natural science gives us a knowledge of physical facts and phenomena, and of the great forces and laws of nature underlying these. This knowledge has in all ages stimulated the most eager curiosity and awakened the spirit of inquiry into physical causes. It has also excited the most wild and extravagant speculations.

The mathematics afford us only the knowledge of the abstract relations of quantity and number, and of certain formulas of analysis. It is by its problems that this science excites the mental activities. Its ideas lie mostly inert in the mind, except when wanted as instruments of calculation.

Language, like mathematics, is mainly concerned with relations; but it is with the relations of ideas and thoughts in all departments of knowledge. The study of language is the study of the connections, as well as of the expression, of thought. Grammar, as J. Stuart Mill has justly observed, is "incipient logic." But language is the *instrument* and the *store-house*, as well as the *vehicle* of thought. It is full of history, philosophy, science and poetry. It powerfully stimulates the thinking processes by the facilities it affords for the manufacture as well as the commerce of thought.

But no knowledge so profoundly stirs and stimulates the human mind as the great questions with which philosophy and history have to do. These questions come down to us from those great central heights of truth, unattainable it may be in their heaven-piercing summits, but still irresistibly attracting all great thinkers, and calling for the mightiest efforts of the human intelligence in the struggle to master their mysterious and still unsolved problems.

It seems too obvious to need further argument that a true educational course must include these four classes of studies, and that if we would send forth a body of thoroughly educated agriculturists, to stand as the peers of the educated men found in other professions, we must give our students the benefits of a course with its full proportionate measure of each of these elements. "It is an ancient and universal observation," said that great thinker and teacher, Sir William Hamilton, "It is an ancient and universal observation, that different studies cultivate the mind to a different development; and as the end of a liberal education is the general and harmonious evolution of its faculties and capacities in their relative subordination, the folly has accordingly been long and generally denounced which would attempt to accomplish this result, by the partial application of certain partial studies." Testimony could be multiplied on this point from the world's greatest thinkers.

It is not necessary that all the branches in each of these great classes of studies be included in the course. Provided that each class is represented in something like its due proportion, we are at liberty to select of two kindred studies of nearly equal disciplinary power, that one which most conduces to the special uses we have in view. In making up a course for the Industrial University, we may wisely and safely depart from the common college curriculum; and, without losing any of its real advantages, may gain much special assistance for our industrial courses.

STUDIES OF THE UNIVERSITY COURSE.

In Physical Sciences, the course should embrace botany, zoology, mineralogy, chemistry, geology and physics, not in the stinted measure and nearly useless manner in which they are usually taught, but with such extent and thoroughness as shall give students a practical comprehension and knowledge of each. The scientific farmer or mechanic should be a good naturalist.

In Mathematics, besides algebra and geometry, the student of agriculture needs trigonometry and land surveying; while the mechanic and civil engineer require also analytical geometry, mechanics and the calculus. These studies, therefore, should find place in this general course.

In language, the course should embrace a thorough study of our own language, its rhetoric and literature.

Of Modern Languages, it should include the French and German, taught with such thoroughness that the student may read them with ease, and converse in them with some facility. The scientific agriculturist ought to be able to avail himself of the fresh discoveries of the French and German men of science. He is shut out from the best scientific thinkers of the age, and from many of the best sources of knowledge, if he can not read the languages of France and Germany. And the prevalent use of these languages in our own country, among large masses of our population, gives to their study an additional value.

The Latin language, both because it enters so largely into our own and other modern languages, and because it is to such an extent the language of science, will demand a place in the course. As an instrument of linguistic culture it greatly surpasses modern languages, and its literature is of perennial value. When well taught, no study more richly rewards the student. The Greek should be afforded, at least as an optional study, to all who desire to pursue it. It will never lose its value in the eyes of the highest grade of scholars.

Mental and Moral Philosophy, Logic, History, Political Ecomomy, Civil Polity and Constitutional Law, will all properly enter into the course as philosophical and speculative studies, and because of their high practical values.

A course, composed of these studies, reaching through four years will fully equal in its disciplinary power the ordinary college course, and be of much more value to the student of the industrial arts.

It seems almost idle to say, we admit, many of these studies are not necessary to the mere practical farmer. Latin will not help a man to hold a plow, nor will mental philosophy teach how to fatten hogs. But we reiterate, the Industrial University is not needed and was not founded for the common education of men, farmers or others. "The liberal and practical education" proposed by Congress will require all the amplitude of study here described.

It is not insisted that all students shall take this general course, though it is strongly recommended. Students may take up special courses without stopping to complete this, just as they may take a medical or law course at any other University, without first graduating from the college course.

The special courses in Agriculture and the Arts will comprehend many of the studies belonging to the general course, and they may be so arranged that a diligent student, of good abilities, while pursuing the regular University course, may also take up and carry forward one of the special technical courses. The studies of the University course being the minimum of study required to entitle the student to regular standing; it will be found that many students can perform successfully more than this minimum.

By further arranging the special courses so as to connect them with the last three years of the University course, and by bringing them, as far as practicable, into the fall and winter session, we may comply with the provision of the law, and also allow students of Agriculture or Horticulture alone, to complete their special studies in a three years' course.

OPTIONAL AND SELECT COURSES.

The opinion gathers currency that students of mature age and experience should be permitted to enter our universities and colleges and select for themselves such studies as they may need, and as they are qualified to pursue successfully with the regular classes in those studies. It may sometimes also occur that persons will desire to enter the university simply to attend some course of lectures, or to attain an insight into some agricultural or other industrial process, as the budding, grafting or pruning of trees, the management of a grapery, etc. Such students should be furnished with all the facilities consistent with the good order of the institution.

QUALIFICATIONS FOR ADMISSION.

The question of the qualifications required for admission to the university is one demanding careful consideration. These requirements should not be so high as to virtually exclude those who might successfully pursue the courses of study, nor so low as to admit those who are unprepared to profit by a residence at the institution, and whose time would be uselessly wasted in the attempt to grasp studies beyond their comprehension.

The law prescribes that "no student shall be admitted to instruction in any of the departments of the University who shall not have attained to the age of fifteen years, and who shall not previously undergo a satisfactory examination in each of the branches ordinarily taught in the common schools of the State." The committee understand this language, not as fixing definitely the qualifications for admission, but only as determining their lowest limit. The trustees may require both a maturer age and a higher grade of scholarship, whenever in their estimation the interests of the State and of the University require it. It would certainly be better if students never entered college under eighteen years of age; but the average age of those applying for admission will doubtless be above this, without any special rule requiring it. Experience shows that students who enter college at a less age than that here indicated, are often injured by being thrown so early into the indiscriminate associations and powerful stimulation of college life. The University is the place for men rather than for mere boys.

It seems requisite that two different sets of qualifications shall be prescribed; the one for students who wish to pursue simply the studies of some select or partial course, and the other for candidates for the regular University courses.

1. QUALIFICATIONS FOR ADMISSION TO SELECT COURSES.

Students may properly be admitted to take some select course, on passing a thorough examination in the common school branches of reading, writing, arithmetic, geography and grammar, and on evidence of sufficient maturity and intelligence to pursue successfully the studies selected by them.

2. ADMISSION TO REGULAR UNIVERSITY COURSES.

While the committee would wish to open the University as widely as possible to the youth of the State, they can not forget that its real utility will depend on establishing and maintaining a high standard of scholarship. As it can not legally do common school work, so neither ought it to undertake to do the work already provided for in the public high schools. It would prove a most sorry blunder if in our too eager desire to popularize the institution, and under pretence of bringing its advantages within the easy reach of all, we should create a gigantic and expensive high school, and, having thus consumed our means, should fail to make any University at all. It is absolutely essential, if the University is to do the higher and scientific work required of it, that it shall leave the preparatory work mainly, if not entirely, to the public high schools and academies of the State; else it may fritter away its funds and its teaching forces, on the mere elementary work already sufficiently provided for, and leave undone all the great work which we ask at its hands for scientific agriculture and industrial arts.

The reasonable construction of the statute is that while the University shall not comprehend the ordinary common school studies, it shall so arrange its terms of admission that the public schools may be able to meet them, and that there be left no unbridged chasm between the body of the State school system and the University at its head.

In the better class of public schools there are now taught, not only Grammar, Geography and Arithmetic, but also Algebra, Geometry, Natural Philosophy, History of the United States, and Human Physiology, and in very many of them the Latin language. All these may properly be prescribed therefore as preparatory studies for the University. They are all so elementary in character as to come within the easy comprehension of students under fifteen years of age; they all need to be studied as preparations for mastering the University course; and they may all be successfully taught in public high schools. In the Latin the quality of the scholarship attained, rather than the quantity of the reading, may wisely be made the test, and the student should be admitted who can construe readily any passage in Cicero's Select Orations, or Virgil's Georgics and Æneid.

The preparatory course above indicated differs from that ordinarily prescribed for admission to colleges, in the omission of the Greek language, and in the extension of the requirements in mathematics and other studies. It is believed that this variation will not only better adapt the preparation to the peculiar character of the University, but will adjust the University much more nearly to the ordinary course of studies now generally taught in our public high schools. These schools universally teach Geometry and Algebra; but only in a few cases teach Greek to any great extent. The grade of scholarship required for admission will thus be made as high as that required at other Universities, though made up of different elements. To make the work of the Industrial University thorough and complete, demands that the preparation for it shall be also full and sufficient.

The argument for an elevated standard of qualifications for admission gains great force from the fact, that until the student has made as much progress as this preparatory course requires, he has not usually formed his purpose and tested his strength and ability to pursue a course of liberal or scientific study. The history of preparatory schools is full of proof that many of those who set out for a college course stop short of the college doors. Science, like scripture, has its "stony ground" hearers, who at first receive the word with joy, but who, when the hot sun of hard study is up, wither away. If our doors must be held open to every half-taught youth who is seized with a sudden ambition to "go to the University," our halls will be flooded annually with fresh hosts of mere tyros, who will stay only long enough to manifest their unfitness for the place, and then go forth to shame the institution whose students they will claim to have been; thus ruining its reputation, after helping to destroy or impair its usefulness.

Among this host of short-lived "students of the Industrial University" the state will look in vain for that long line of graduates—the ripe and scholarly leaders in her agriculture and her great industries—which she has hoped to see proceed annually from the university halls.

The committee are confident that no person who properly considers the amount of more important work which the university has to accomplish, will wish to see its forces diverted to the teaching of these elementary branches which the high schools may properly claim as their own ground; and certainly no one who desires the success of the university, as a great scientific and industrial college, will wish to see students entering its classes with less preparation than is here prescribed.

It needs to be repeated that this does not forbid students of suitable maturity and experience to come to the university to take a few select studies, without passing an examination in Latin and the higher mathematics named.

HONORARY SCHOLARSHIPS.

The law for the organization of the university provides that "each county in the state shall be entitled to one honorary scholarship in the university, for the benefit of the descendants of soldiers and seamen who served in the armies and navies of the United States during the late rebellion; preference being given to the children of such soldiers and seaman as are deceased or disabled; and the board of trustees may from time to time add to the number of honorary scholarships when, in their judgment, such additions will not embarrass the finances of the university; nor need these additions be confined to the descendants of soldiers or seamen. Such scholarships to be filled by transfer from the common schools of said county of such pupils as shall, upon public examination, to be conducted as the board of trustees of the university may determine, be decided to have attained the greatest proficiency in the branches of learning usually taught in the common schools, and who shall be of good moral character and not less than fifteen years of age." These scholarships entitle the incumbents to free tuition for three years.

The committee recommend that the Regent, in connection with the Superintendent of Public Instruction, prepare examination papers, and transmit the same to the county superintendent of schools in each county, who, with other examiners, appointed by the Regent and Superintendent, will see that the examinations are properly conducted, and will return the papers, with the written answers of the several candidates and with such testimonials as they may present, to the Regent, who shall determine on the papers and notify the successful candidates of their appointment.

A competitive examination, thus uniform in character and thus fairly conducted, can not but react with a most healthful stimulation upon the public school interests of the state; and this stimulation will be increased by a publication of the names of the schools in which the successful candidates were prepared, and the teachers by whom they were taught. In case any counties shall neglect to send students on their scholarships, the Regent may be authorized to award such scholarships, for the year, to suitable candidates from other counties.

CHARGES FOR TUITION, AND OTHER EXPENSES.

The committee would rejoice if the condition of our funds and the provisions of the law would permit the University to be made free to all citizens of the State, and they cordially recommend that its tuition be made thus free at the earliest practicable moment; and that from the outset the charges be made as light as as consistent with justice to the institution itself.

The charges in American Colleges range from a few dollars per annum to several hundreds. In Yale College the annual fees amount to $85. The annual fees at Harvard are $133. At the Michigan University each student pays a matriculation fee of $10, and an annual fee of $5. At the Michigan Agricultural College the tuition is free for citizens of the State. Students from other States pay $20 per annum. All students pay a matriculation fee of $5. The proposed fees for the Cornell University are $20 a year for tuition; matriculation fee $15.

The committee recommend that the academic year be divided into two semi-annual sessions, as nearly equal as may be, and that the tuition and other fees for each session be fixed at the following rates:

For tuition to students from other States, $10 per term	$20 per annum
For incidentals, care and warming of public rooms, etc., $5 per term	10 " "
For room rent, $6 per term	12 " "

They recommend, also, that a matriculation fee of $10 be charged to each student on first entering the institution. This fee is never charged a second time, but once paid, entitles the student to all the privileges of membership at any time thereafter.

Students on the "honorary scholarships" will pay the matriculation fee and charges for room rent and incidentals, but will be charged nothing for tuition.

BOARDING DEPARTMENT.

The building is provided with the necessary rooms for a boarding department. It is believed that in a short time we may wholly dispense with this department, even if it must be opened at the outset. Suitable boarding houses will doubtless soon spring up in the neighborhood, and the rooms in the University building may be appropriated to more public and proper uses.

STUDENTS' ROOMS.

There are in the University buildings sixty-six rooms designed for students' dormitories, each dormitory being calculated to accommodate two students. These rooms are without furniture. It is customary to leave students to provide their own furniture, as they will ordinarily take better care of their own property than they will of that belonging to a public institution.

MANUAL LABOR SYSTEM.

One of the most important and difficult questions concerning the organization of the University is that of the introduction of the manual labor system. It is true that the attempt to connect manual labor with schools has in many instances failed; but the nature and extent of this failure have not been generally understood. It has not failed because the students were unwilling to work, nor because the work was injurious either to their health or culture. It has simply failed to pay. The labor of students was found unprofitable.

The high success and utility of the labor system, as practiced at the Michigan Agricultural College, has, in the minds of your committee, fully demonstrated its feasibility and value; and they would heartily recommend its adoption here, provided similar conditions can be secured. There, each student is required by law to work three hours a day, unless excused on account of sickness. The professors accompany the students to the garden or field, and participate in and direct the work, which is made to illustrate the principles taught in the lecture rooms. Wages, according to the value of the work done, not exceeding seven and a-half cents an hour, are allowed the student, and he is thus enabled to pay a considerable part of the expense of his schooling by his labor. Even there the work has never yet proved remunerative to the institution, though it annually approaches nearer this result.

It should be added that the manual labor system, as practiced at the above named institution, has been carefully inspected by gentlemen sent from several of the eastern States, and has been warmly commended in their published reports, as eminently satisfactory and successful.

The chief advantages of the labor system are these:

1. It promotes the physical health and development of the student.
2. It cultivates habits of industry, and, keeping the student inured to muscular effort, renders his return to the farm, or other physical labor, natural and easy. This is a point of much importance, if we wish successfully to turn the tides of educated life into the industrial employments.
3. When made, as in the agricultural course, to bear upon the studies pursued, it creates a practical interest in, and comprehension of, those studies which cannot be obtained by mere abstract study.
4. When pursued, as here recommended, in the society of intelligent class-mates and teachers, and lighted with a knowledge of the reason of every process, it is not only pleasant, but comes to be seen as noble and dignified; and thus the sentiment of honor to labor is deeply implanted in the mind.
5. It aids the student to pay his own way, and cultivates in him the feeling of manly independence.

These considerations are so important that they incline us to recommend its introduction, even though it should fail to pay all the expenses attending it. But, if proper care is taken not to establish too high a

—2

rate of compensation, the Committee are not without hope that no loss need result, even if no profit is gained.

APPARATUS OF ILLUSTRATION AND INSTRUCTION.

Each department in the University will require, besides the general cabinets or collections, some means of illustration and instruction peculiar to itself. For general study of the natural sciences there will be needed full and well classified collections of specimens in mineralogy and geology, in botany and in the various branches of zoology.

The departments of agriculture and horticulture will require in addition, cabinets of seeds, grasses, grains and fruits; models or drawings of farming and garden implements, of farm buildings, and plans of farms, gardens, celebrated parks, and landscape gardens, etc.; and specimens and drawings of various breeds of domestic animals.

The department of mechanics and civil engineering, will demand a cabinet of models and drawings of machinery, architectural plans, plans of roads, bridges and other structures, and specimens of building materials, as the various woods, marbles, granites and more common building stones.

The military department will require its specimens or drawings of the various kinds of arms and military structures, together with plans of celebrated battle-fields, sieges, encampments, etc.

The department of fine arts will require casts, photographs or engravings of the great master-pieces in art. These may be obtained at reasonable rates, and original drawings, paintings and sculptures will, in due time be added. The healthful, refining and stimulating influence of such collections on the minds of the young, must be seen to be properly appreciated.

The common working apparatus of instruction must embrace a good set of chemical and philosophical apparatus. The prominence due to chemistry in such an institution as this, will demand, at the earliest practicable day, a separate and suitable building for a chemical laboratory, such as exists at Harvard, Yale and Amherst, and at the Michigan University.

The experimental farms, orchards and gardens, with the several stock barns, yards, pens, etc.; the mechanic shops, tools and machinery; the military arms and parade grounds; the engineer's tools, and the model counting house, will furnish the fitting apparatus for teaching in the several leading departments of special instruction.

As the collection of cabinets is a work of years, it is important that it begin at once, and that applications for duplicate specimens, casts, etc., be made as early as practicable, wherever they may be obtained. The friends of the University in the various sections of the State would doubtless donate many specimens, if a brief circular, containing a statement of our wants, and instructions for packing and forwarding, were sent out.

FACULTY.

The committee were also instructed "to suggest a faculty" for the University. In the entire work of organizing the institution, there is no more difficult or important part than this. On the character and ability of its faculty, will the character and success of the University depend, more than upon all other circumstances taken together. Buildings, cabinets, libraries and rich endowments will be all in vain, if the living agents—the professors—be not men of ripe attainments, fine culture and eminent teaching powers.

Numerous applications have already flowed in upon the committee, but the time has been quite too brief, since the last meeting of the board, to allow any such careful and extensive inquiries as would justify the committee in presenting any names at this time. Self-nominated candidates will always be abundant, but the men we want will need to be sought for as with lighted candles. The incumbent of a professor's chair should be no ordinary man. In this, its chief seat of learning, in which it proposes to provide for the highest education of its sons, and from which, as a great center of science, it seeks to diffuse light to all the great fields of its industries, the State needs men of the highest type as scholars and as men. The qualifications of every candidate for a professorship must be rigidly scrutinized without fear or favor; and none but men of tried and proven ability must be admitted to a place. Older and ordinary colleges may do with second rate men; this University can only succeed with the best men.

A good college professor should have the three-fold qualification of eminent and extensive scholarship, at least in his department; thoroughly tested ability to teach; and high-toned, gentlemanly character and culture. The first two are indispensable qualifications; the third will never be overlooked by those who have marked how inevitably and ineffaceably the teacher impresses his manners and habits upon his pupils. If culture is the better part of education, high-toned character and genuine courtesy of manner and feeling are the better part of culture.

The number of professors must depend upon the extent of the endowments and the consequent ability to pay salaries. Until the trustees shall determine upon the disposition of the land scrip, and thus approximately determine the prospective extent of its funds, this question of the numerical force of the faculty must remain unsettled.

The corps of instruction may properly embrace four classes of teachers: 1st. *Professors*, or principal instructors in each department of study. 2d. *Assistant Professors*—younger, or less accomplished teachers, employed in sub-departments, or to aid in departments in which the work cannot be fully done by one man. 3d. *Lecturers*, or non-resident Professors—men eminent in some specialty of art or science, who may be employed to visit the University at specified seasons, and give courses of lectures. 4th. *Tutors*, or young men, employed temporarily to give instruction in the more elementary studies.

The committee would indicate the following as among the more important departments or chairs of instruction:

1. The Professorship of Practical and Theoretical Agriculture.
2. " " of Horticulture.
3. " " of Analytical and Practical Mechanics.
4. " " of Military Tactics and Engineering.
5. " " of Civil Engineering.
6. " " of Botany and Vegetable Physiology.

7. The Professorship of Zoology and Animal Physiology.
8. " " of Mathematics.
9. " " of Chemistry.
10. " " of Geology, Mineralogy and Physical Geography.
11. " " of English Language and Literature.
12. " " of Modern Languages.
13. " " of Ancient Languages.
14. " " of History and Social Science.
15. " " of Mental and Moral Philosophy.

In addition to these, the committee would suggest the following lectureships:

1. The Lectureship of Veterinary Science.
2. " " of Commercial Science.
3. " " of Human Anatomy, Physiology and Hygiene.
4. " " of Constitutional, Commercial and Rural Law.

Several of these departments may, at the outset, be represented by the same man. The professor of botany may also be professor of horticulture; and the professor of zoology may fill, likewise, the chair of practical agriculture. Civil and military engineering may be united in one chair; and the professor of chemistry may teach also mineralogy or meteorology.

The professor of Practical Agriculture should be the superintendent of the experimental farm, with such foremen and other laborers under him as may be necessary to carry out his plans. The farm is his laboratory and apparatus of instruction, by which he illustrates the scientific principles and theories which he teaches, and demonstrates both the truth and the value of his doctrines. His plans for the treatment of each field and crop, and for the several experiments to be tried, should be submitted to the Regent and Faculty, and after careful discussion and final adoption by them, or by the Executive committee, should be put on record as the settled plan for that season, to be carried out under the careful supervision of the superintendent, and its progress and results fully recorded in the farm record.

In like manner, the professor of Horticulture should be superintendent of the gardens and ornamental grounds, and should, in the same way, present to the Faculty for their discussion and approval, his plans for the management of such grounds and gardens. He, too, when necessary, may be aided in his work by a foreman and other laborers. The students, in their labors in the gardens or on the farm, will be under the guidance of the professors whose instructions those labors are designed to illustrate and apply; and thus the lecture room and the field practice will teach the same truths, and throw upon each other the light of a mutual illustration.

The professor of Mechanics may have under his care such shops as may be needed on the grounds for purposes of repairs, or of such new constructions of any kind as may be easily made. With a small steam or caloric engine as a motor power, there may be run a variety of common machinery, such as the turning lathe, circular saws, mills for grinding feed, etc., and threshing and other machines, which will enable the instructor in this department to furnish practical illustration of the principles of mechanics. The truth taught to the eye is much more easily understood and remembered than that which is stated in mere words. Every where the practical methods should supplement and impress the theoretical instruction.

At the Michigan Agricultural College the students repair the farm tools and make many of them. Several important improvements in farming implements have already originated there, though they have, as yet, no fully provided mechanical department. Students are also employed in the erection of new buildings as they are needed, and they are said to soon excel common workmen in the excellence of their work.

CONCLUSION.

In presenting this preliminary report, the committee purposely hold in reserve several points of much interest and importance, which they hope to be able to present finally in a much more definite and satisfactory form than can be done with the information now in hand. Maturer consideration than the time now allowed them has permitted, may also lead to some modification of certain of the points here presented.

Fully comprehending the great magnitude and the immeasurable importance of the enterprise which they are seeking to shape into life and power, they can only bespeak for it the wise support and the just forbearance of all good and intelligent citizens.

An industrial university such as we are planning is, in a large part, without precedent or example. The field of its labors is as yet almost untracked in its widest stretches. The very classes for whom its benefits are designed, are as yet not half persuaded of the importance and real value of those benefits. The farmers and mechanics, accustomed to regard higher education as needful and desirable only for professional men, and almost wholly incredulous as to the utility of science in its applications to their work, will look with slow-coming faith upon a university which proposes to make farming a scientific employment, and to lift mechanics into a learned profession. They have, in many cases, yet to be convinced that a highly cultured mind may be linked to a brawny hand, and that a classical scholar may feel at home in a workshop; aye! and find use for all his scholarship and taste in the successful practice of his art.

But the age is propitious. The working masses of mankind are waking to their needs, and calling for light. The thunder of the machinery by the side of which they toil, and the magic power of the new processes of arts which they daily employ, have roused the long slumbering power of thought. Brains are coming into use and honor in all the fields of human labor, and brains will speedily demand light and knowledge. In an age of learning, the farmer and the mechanic will soon come to covet the rich heritages of science for their sons. Already the children of the laboring classes are crowding the public high schools. They will not stop there. The University lies the next step beyond. They will crowd to its doors; and soon will begin to issue from its halls that long column, with its yearly additions, of graduates with broad brows, and science-lighted brains, bearing back to the farms andthe workshops an intelligent skill and power, to invoke new and unwonted fruitfulness from the soil and from the mechanic's art. "If

I had fifty sons," said a farmer who had reluctantly permitted his eldest boy to take a course at an agricultural college, and now brought his youngest to the same college, "If I had fifty sons they should all go to this college, for my boy, who graduated here, farms so much better than I ever did, skillful as I thought myself, that he is getting rich from his half of the crops he raises on my land, and I live like a prince on the remainder."

And the light of high and classic learning will be found as beautiful and becoming when it shines in an educated farmer's home, as when it gilds the residence of the graduated lawyer or physician. Rich libraries are already seen in the houses of some of our leading agriculturists, and no one has found that they hinder the growth of harvests, or unfit the hand of the reaper. When our Industrial University shall have come fully into its work, these libraries will be increased in number, and there will gather around the firesides in our farm houses, and in the homes of our master mechanics, groups of cultivated and intelligent people, the peers in knowledge, refinement and power of the best and bravest in the land.

And what richer growths shall yet start from these magnificent prairies to repay the farmer's toil, and what more splendid achievements shall yet spring from our myriad-handed mechanic art—what more beautiful bloom in our gardens, and more delicious fruits from our orchards—what more tasteful and convenient homes from our architecture, and what grander and more abundant products from our multiplying manufactories—what nobler forms of civilization to grace our free institution, and what better types of manhood to tell of the blessings of liberty and learning, when education shall have fully achieved this last triumph, and carried her victorious banner of light down into the fields where the toiling millions of mankind must still, by the stern but beneficent ordination of Heaven, "eat their bread in the sweat of their brows."

J. M. GREGORY,
NEWTON BATEMAN,
MASON BRAYMAN,
S. S. HAYES,
WILLARD C. FLAGG, } *Committee.*

www.ingramcontent.com/pod-product-compliance
Lightning Source LLC
La Vergne TN
LVHW020634110826
845149LV00004B/1181

* 9 7 8 1 4 1 8 1 9 1 5 6 6 *